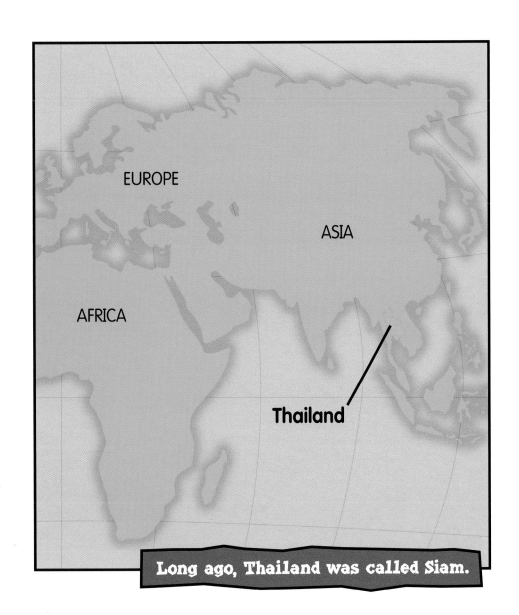

EUROPE

ASIA

AFRICA

Thailand

Long ago, Thailand was called Siam.

Why are Siamese cats called "royal cats of Siam" and "palace cats"? Siam's kings and queens kept Siamese cats. These cats may have guarded Siam's palaces and temples, too.

The Siam people thought their Siamese cats were special.

The First Siamese Cat In America

Lucy Webb Hayes

The first Siamese cat came to America in the late 1800s. It was a female cat named Siam. This cat was a gift from someone in Siam for Lucy Webb Hayes. She was President Hayes's wife.

What They Are Like

Siamese cats are smart, loving, and playful. They enjoy attention and may meow often. Some Siamese cats love to sit on people's shoulders. Other Siamese cats love to sit on a person's lap. Every Siamese cat is special in its own way.

Siamese cats make great pets.

Classic Siamese Colors

Siamese cats have light-colored bodies and darker **points**. These points are a cat's face, ears, feet, and tail.

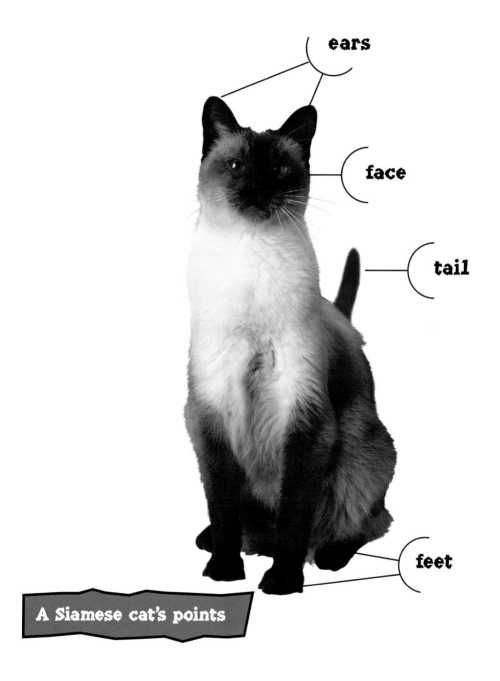

ears

face

tail

feet

A Siamese cat's points

There are four classic Siamese cat colors. Seal-point Siamese cats are cream-colored with dark brown **points**. Chocolate-point Siamese cats have dark brown points, too. Blue-point Siamese cats have blue-gray points. Lilac-point Siamese cats are off-white with pinkish-gray points.

Seal-point Siamese

Chocolate-point Siamese

Blue-point Siamese

Lilac-point Siamese

Show Cats

At cat shows, judges try to find the best-looking cats. These judges look for special things in a Siamese cat. They look for blue, almond-shaped eyes and large, pointed ears. A Siamese cat's head must be triangle-shaped, not round. A long, slender body with a long, thin tail is important, too.

This cat has the triangle-shaped head that judges look for.

The Mixed Siamese

Close relatives of the Siamese cat may have colored **points**. But they may not have the classic Siamese colors. These part-Siamese cats are called **colorpoint shorthairs**.

Colorpoint shorthair cats can have red or cream points. Their points can be a mix of **tortoiseshell** colors, too. Tortie-point cats have brown points mixed with red, cream, or both. Another colorpoint shorthair is the lynx-point cat. It has striped points.

Colorpoint shorthair with red points

Seal-point Siamese

Care

Siamese cats are clean animals. They lick themselves to stay clean. This is called **grooming**.

You should brush your cat once a week. Use a small, rubber brush. Brushing removes loose hair that could lead to **hair balls**.

Cats need food and fresh water everyday. Cats also need a **litter box**. Clean your cat's litter box every day.

Siamese house cats
need a litter box.

Kittens

As many as six kittens may be born in a **litter**. Siamese cats are born with white fur. Their **point** colors may start to show during the first year.

Newborn kittens are blind. After a few weeks, they can see. Three-week-old kittens will begin to crawl and play. Kittens need their mother's milk. They should stay with her for 12 weeks. It takes six to eight months for kittens to become adult cats.

This Siamese kitten's point colors have started to show.

Important Words

colorpoint shorthairs part-Siamese cats that have different color points.

groom to clean and care for.

hair ball hair that collects in a cat's stomach after grooming.

litter a group of kittens born at one time.

litter box a place for house cats to leave their waste.

points body parts of a Siamese cat (face, ears, feet, and tail) that have darker hair.

tortoiseshell describes a cat's mixed coat of colors: black or brown, red, and sometimes cream.

Web Sites

The Cat Fanciers' Association

www.cfainc.org
Learn about the different breeds of cats.

I Love Cats.com

www.I-Love-Cats.com
Cat facts, games, pictures, and links to other
cat sites can be found here.

Legends and History of the Siamese Cat

www.Siamesekitties.com/infopage.html
Read about the history of the Siamese cat and
legends of its past.

Index